MILET
WORDWISE

Telling Tails

Fun with Homonyms

Laura Hambleton & Sedat Turhan

Illustrated by Laura Hambleton

Milet Publishing, LLC
333 North Michigan Avenue
Suite 530
Chicago, IL 60601
info@milet.com
www.milet.com

Telling Tails: Fun with Homonyms
Text by Laura Hambleton and Sedat Turhan
Illustrations by Laura Hambleton

First published by Milet Publishing, LLC in 2006

ISBN-13: 978 1 84059 498 0
ISBN-10: 1 84059 498 5

Printed and bound in China

Please see our website **www.milet.com**
for other Milet Wordwise titles.

Telling Tails

Fun with Homonyms

Laura Hambleton & Sedat Turhan
Illustrated by Laura Hambleton

Does the forest have **fur**trees?

Would you
like to eat
a chocolate

desert?

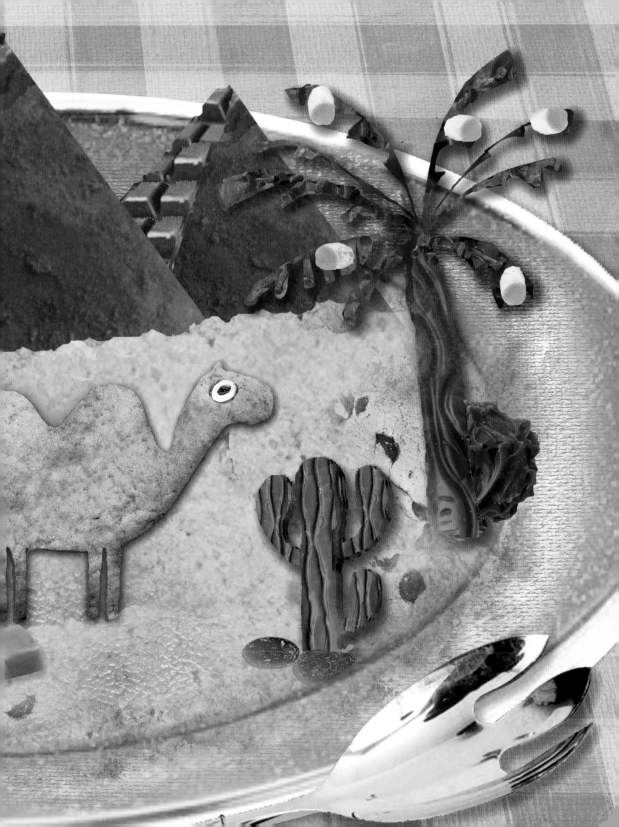

I'm washing
my
hare.

What a big **wail**!

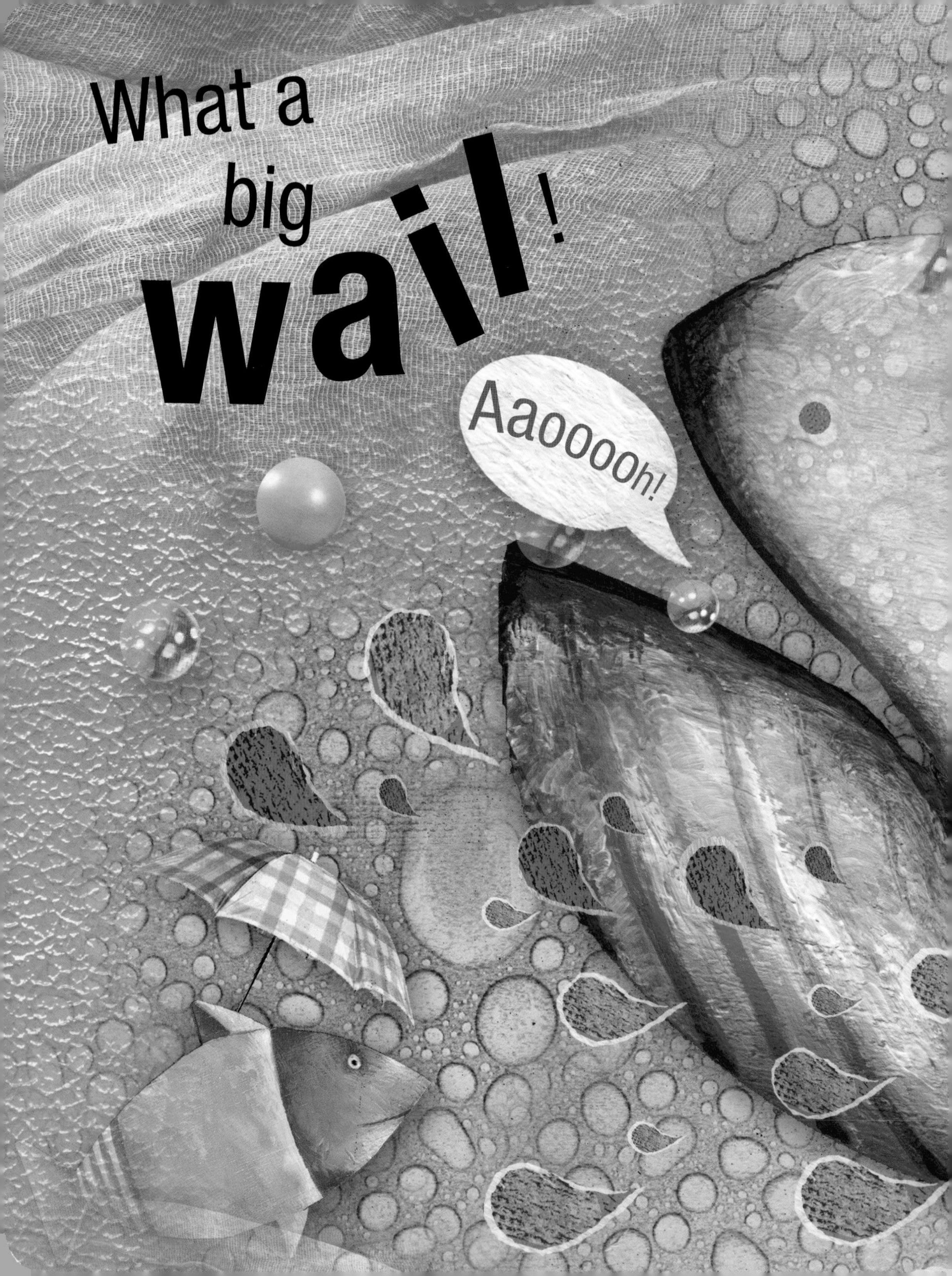

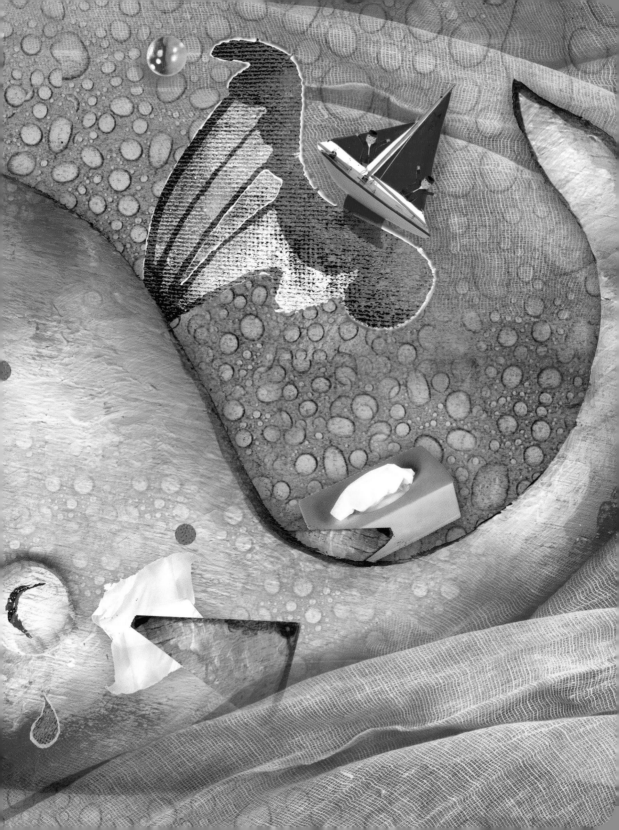

I need **flower** for my cake.

The tap has sprung a **leek**.

Let's take
a trip on a
fairy!

I'm going to **rap** presents.

I wonder how the clouds **reign**.

What a wonderful **tale**!

HomOnyms

A homonym is a word that sounds the same as another word but has a different meaning.

1. horse   hoarse   *errgghh!*

2. fur   fir

3. desert   dessert

4. hare   hair

5. wail   whale

6   flower   flour

7   leek   leak

8   fairy   ferry

9   wrap   rap

10   reign   rain

11   tale   tail

Other titles in the **Milet Wordwise** series

Strawberry Bullfrog: Fun with Compound Words
Monkey Business: Fun with Idioms
Jump, Jog, Leapfrog: Fun with Action Words

Other Milet books by the creators of
Telling Tails: Fun with Homonyms

Laura Hambleton

English with Abby and Zak
Chameleon Races
Chameleon Swims
Welcome to Lizard Lounge
How Bees Be
I'm Afraid too!

Sedat Turhan

Milet Flashwords
Milet Mini Picture Dictionary
Milet Picture Dictionary

www.milet.com